A money timeline

2250 BC

Cappadocia (in present-day Turkey) is the first state to guarantee the quality of silver ingots, increasing their acceptance as money.

9000 BC

Livestock, especially cattle, is used as a form of exchange.

AD 806

Paper money is invented in China.

3000 BC

Banking begins in Babylonia. Gold is placed in temples and priests issue loans.

1232

The florin, a gold coin minted in Florence, Italy, becomes a widely accepted currency in Europe.

600 BC

King Alyattes of Lydia is the first monarch to mint coins of a standard weight.

1950

Diners Club launches the first credit card.

1999

Banks start offering mobile banking, using the first smartphones.

1661

Europe's first banknotes are issued, in Sweden.

1981

Online banking begins when a New York bank offers home banking services using the Videotex system.

1860

Western Union makes the first electronic funds transfer (EFT), marking the birth of e-money.

Security features on banknotes

PLEASE NOTE: This is a fictitious banknote. Copying real banknotes is against the law.

Feel of the paper: *Banknotes are printed on special paper that feels different from ordinary paper.*

Metallic thread: *This appears as silver dashes. If you hold the note up to the light, it appears as a continuous line.*

Raised print: *Run your finger across the surface to feel the areas of embossed print.*

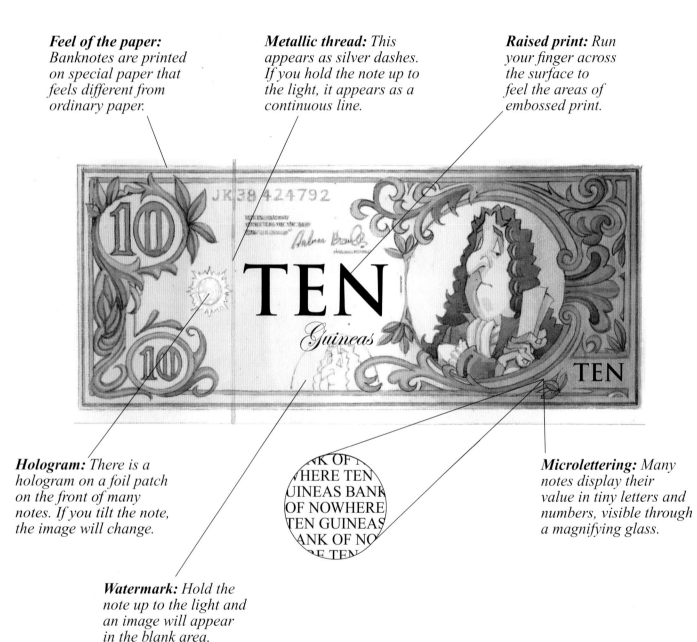

Hologram: *There is a hologram on a foil patch on the front of many notes. If you tilt the note, the image will change.*

Microlettering: *Many notes display their value in tiny letters and numbers, visible through a magnifying glass.*

Watermark: *Hold the note up to the light and an image will appear in the blank area.*

Author:

Alex Woolf studied history at Essex University, England. He is the author of over 60 books for children, including *You Wouldn't Want to Live Without Books!*, *You Wouldn't Want to Live Without Fire!* and *You Wouldn't Want to Live Without Soap!*

Artist:

David Antram was born in Brighton, England, in 1958. He studied at Eastbourne College of Art and then worked in advertising for 15 years before becoming a full-time artist. He has illustrated many children's non-fiction books.

Series creator:

David Salariya was born in Dundee, Scotland. He has illustrated a wide range of books and has created and designed many new series for publishers in the UK and overseas. David established The Salariya Book Company in 1989. He lives in Brighton with his wife, illustrator Shirley Willis, and their son Jonathan.

Editor: **Stephen Haynes**

Editorial Assistant: **Mark Williams**

Published in Great Britain in MMXVI by
Book House, an imprint of
The Salariya Book Company Ltd
25 Marlborough Place, Brighton BN1 1UB
www.salariya.com
www.book-house.co.uk
ISBN: 978-1-910184-93-6

3 5 7 9 8 6 4 2

A CIP catalogue record for this book is available from the British Library.

Printed and bound in China.
Reprinted in MMXVII.

Visit
www.salariya.com
for our online catalogue and
free fun stuff.

You Wouldn't Want to Live Without™
Money!

Written by
Alex Woolf

Illustrated by
David Antram

Series created by
David Salariya

BOOK HOUSE
a SALARIYA *imprint*

Contents

Introduction

Can you imagine what life would be like if we didn't have money? How would we get the food, clothing and other things we need? Money is incredibly useful and it's hard to picture our world without it. But money didn't always exist. It had to be invented. And, since then, it has taken many different forms. Cows, bronze 'spades' and knives have all been used as money. You can imagine how the invention of coins and paper money made things a bit easier! But even these forms of money may be disappearing. Already, money is becoming invisible, moving from one place to another with the click of a mouse or the scan of a card. This book traces the history of money and looks at the many ways in which it has transformed our world.

Cow

Chinese spade money

Credit and debit cards

E-money

Notes and coins

Can you bear to barter?

Imagine living in a world before money. How do you pay for the things you need? If you're a fruit grower and you need a spear, you must go to a spear maker and offer him some of your produce as payment. This system is called bartering, and it has its drawbacks. You have to find someone who has what you want, but also wants what you have. Also, every purchase takes time as there's no agreed value for the goods you're trying to swap. No-one can say, for example, whether a basket of apples is a fair price for a spear.

POTLATCH. In a custom called potlatch, leaders of the Chinook people in North America tried to outdo each other with exchanges of elaborate gifts and feasts. This was another way of sharing out goods without using money.

EXPLORERS. Bartering didn't end with the invention of money. During the 15th to 18th centuries, European explorers bartered with natives in the places they visited.

IN THE GREAT DEPRESSION of the 1930s, people resorted to bartering to get food and clothing. Some even swapped bread and sausages for tickets to the theatre.

BARTERING TODAY. Online 'swap markets' are global, so there's more chance of finding someone who wants what you have and has what you want!

Are you in the mood for money?

You are a cattle herder living in the Middle East in around 9000 BC. You wish to buy grain, stone tools and pottery from others in your village. But first you must work out how much these things are worth. After much talk, you all agree on prices for the grain, the stone tools and the pottery. You work this out by deciding how many of these things you could buy with one cow. The cow has become a 'unit of value' in your village. It has become the first *money*.

It's rather small.

COMMODITY MONEY. Early money was valued because of what it was. For example, a cow is valued for its milk and meat. This is called 'commodity money'.

WEAPONS were often used as money in ancient times. Axes were exchanged in the Americas, and large bronze knives were used in ancient China. They must have been dangerous to carry around!

I wish I had more fingers.

COWRIE SHELLS were used as an early form of money in China, India and Africa. Their advantage was that they were hard to forge, and, unlike cows, they didn't die.

RING MONEY. The ancient Egyptians liked to wear their wealth on their fingers. They paid for things with bronze, silver or gold rings.

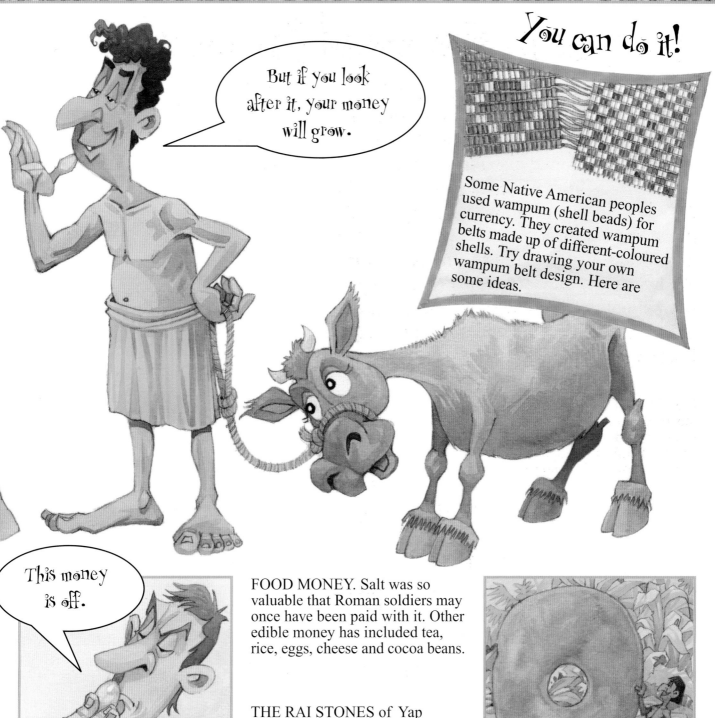

But if you look after it, your money will grow.

Some Native American peoples used wampum (shell beads) for currency. They created wampum belts made up of different-coloured shells. Try drawing your own wampum belt design. Here are some ideas.

This money is off.

FOOD MONEY. Salt was so valuable that Roman soldiers may once have been paid with it. Other edible money has included tea, rice, eggs, cheese and cocoa beans.

THE RAI STONES of Yap Island in the Pacific are the world's biggest money. At up to 3.6 metres (12 feet) across and weighing several tonnes, they are rarely moved.

9

Can you count on coins?

You are a shopkeeper living in Sardis, capital of Lydia (now western Turkey), in 600 BC. Your king, Alyattes, has done something completely new in history: he has minted official coins containing a standard weight of metal. They are made from electrum, a mixture of silver and gold, and are stamped with a roaring lion. For the first time, there is now a standard currency, recognised throughout the kingdom. The only problem: some people might skim off some of the precious metal from their coins and pay you with 'debased' money. You keep a set of scales in your shop to weigh the coins you receive, to make sure your customers aren't cheating you.

THE CHINESE were using coins as early as 770 BC, but these were knife- or spade-shaped. The first round Chinese coins had holes in the centre and appeared in 350 BC.

LYDIA'S CURRENCY helped make it one of the richest states in the ancient world. The phrase 'rich as Croesus' refers to the Lydian king, Alyattes' son, who minted the first gold coins.

Your coins are too light.

Your goods are too expensive.

You can do it!

Sometimes the gold or silver in coins might be mixed with harder, less valuable metals. You can test the purity of a coin by rubbing it on a touchstone – a stone tablet with a finely grained surface on which soft metals leave a visible mark.

THE FIRST COIN minted in Lydia showed a roaring lion. Others showed owls and snakes. The image indicated the weight and value of the coin.

CLIPPING. Criminals would sometimes 'clip' or shave the edges off coins. These precious metal fragments could be melted down to make fake coins.

DEBASEMENT. Criminals might saw a coin in half, take out a plug of metal from the inside, fill the hole with inferior metal, then weld the two halves back together.

11

Are you prepared for paper?

OFFICIAL PAPER CURRENCY began circulating in China in the late 900s AD. By 1023 the notes had become as accepted as coins.

You are a Chinese silk merchant in the year 806 AD. You've just been paid for a shipment of silk to the imperial palace. But instead of copper coins, they've paid you with… paper. An official explains that it is far more convenient to send paper certificates than coins over long distances. You can convert them into coins when you visit the palace. You soon get used to the paper money. You nickname it 'flying cash' because of its tendency to blow away. Soon you start paying other merchants with flying cash, almost as though it were real money.

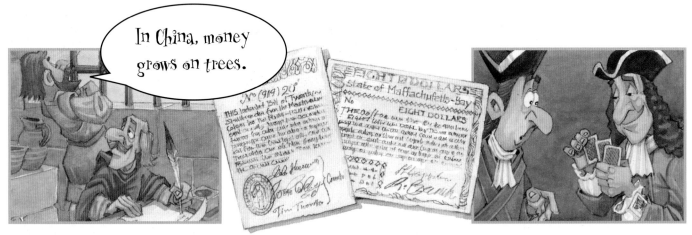

In China, money grows on trees.

MARCO POLO, from Venice in Italy, visited China in the 1200s. He brought back tales of how the Chinese turn the bark of trees into paper for use as money.

MASSACHUSETTS MONEY. The first Western government to issue paper currency was the Massachusetts Bay Colony in North America, in the 1690s.

PLAYING-CARD MONEY. In 1685, when the French colony of Canada briefly ran out of coins, the governor began paying his soldiers in playing cards.

Are you better off with banking?

You are an *argentarius* (banker) living in Rome in 325 BC. You set up your stall in the public forum, or marketplace. You change foreign merchants' money into Roman coins and you lend money to those who need it, charging them a regular sum (interest). You also pay interest to those who deposit money with you. One of your fellow bankers has got into trouble. He has loaned money to someone and they can't pay it back. Now he can't afford to pay interest to his depositors. He is bankrupt.

> I've struck gold with this banking business.

GOLDSMITHS became the first English bankers in 1640. They provided a safe place to store gold after King Charles I started seizing gold from the Royal Mint.

> If I cheat you, he'll strike me down!

TEMPLE BANKS. The very earliest banks were in temples because they were less likely to be robbed. Babylonian priests (above) even made loans.

THE MEDICI were a wealthy banking family from Florence, Italy, in the late Middle Ages. They grew so powerful that four of their members became pope.

> I've come for a blessing... and a loan.

Whoopee! Napoleon lost at Waterloo!

ROTHSCHILDS. The Rothschild banking dynasty began during the Napoleonic wars, helping to finance Napoleon's enemies. They kept up with events by using carrier pigeons.

Top tip

If you want to be a successful banker, be careful who you lend money to. In the 1340s, King Edward III of England borrowed so much money to fund his war against France that he bankrupted two Florentine banking dynasties.

Can I interest you in a loan?

Only if your interest is low.

Argentarius

15

Would you care for some credit?

It's the early 12th century and you are tax collector to King Henry I of England. For every taxpayer you create a notched piece of wood called a tally stick. The notches show how much tax they owe. You split the tally stick down the middle and give one half to the taxpayer, keeping the other half for yourself. With the matching notches on both halves, there's no question how much tax is owed. But some are late paying their taxes and the king is running out of money. So you start using the tally sticks to pay the king's debts. You have invented an early form of credit.

It doesn't look like money.

Credit comes from the Latin word credo, meaning 'I believe'.

It's as good as money...

...so long as the buyer eventually pays up.

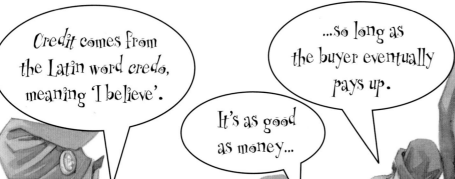

WHAT IS CREDIT? When a customer receives goods before paying for them, because the seller trusts that payment will be made later, this is called credit.

BILLS OF EXCHANGE were a promise to pay later. In the 1500s Italian merchants bought and sold goods with these bills, or swapped them for money at a bank.

Here's your bill.

And here's an IOU.

AN IOU is a kind of credit, based on the words 'I owe you'. First used in 1795, it's a written statement from a debtor saying that he owes an amount of money, but doesn't say when it will be repaid.

Are you arguing with the king?

How it works

Credit cards allow people to borrow money to buy things. The credit card provider charges interest until the borrowed money is paid back.

Oops!

COINS AND PLATES. In the 1860s, shops began offering celluloid or metal coins as credit tokens. In the 1920s, these were replaced with little metal plates called charga-plates.

FRANK McNAMARA was dining out in New York in 1949 when he realised he'd left his wallet at home. This gave him the idea for the Diners Club Card, the first popular credit card.

17

Dare you dice with debt?

t is the late 14th century. You have been thrown into London's Marshalsea prison for failing to pay your debts. All that you own has been sold to pay your creditors. You will stay here until you or your family can pay back the rest of what you owe. You live in a filthy communal cell alongside other debtors. If you're lucky, you'll be released to become an indentured servant to one of your creditors, and you'll be able to work off your debts through labour. But it's just as likely that you'll die here in prison from disease or starvation.

How can I pay back what I owe if I'm stuck in here?

DEBT SLAVES. In early Roman times, a person could offer himself as security for a loan. Failure to repay meant slavery.

Top tip

Be careful with your money. Before you buy anything, make sure you can afford it. Pay off any debts as soon as you can.

Traditional pawnbroker's sign

NOSE TAX. During the 800s AD, Danish rulers in Ireland would slit the noses of those who failed to pay their taxes. This *may* be the origin of the saying 'to pay through the nose'.

PAWNBROKERS lend money at interest on the security of a valuable object. If the debt is not repaid, they keep the object. They first appeared in China 3,000 years ago, and still exist today.

LOAN SHARKS prey on debtors by offering loans at extremely high interest rates. They sometimes resort to violence or blackmail to force debtors to repay the loans.

19

On and off

1816: Britain officially adopts the gold standard. Others soon follow. It fixes the value of currencies to gold and helps keep prices stable.

> We'll just have to print more money.

1914: The gold standard ends because governments' need to print money to pay for World War I is thwarted by a finite gold supply.

US BULLION   DEPOSITORY

1946: The gold standard returns. Governments can trade their currencies for US gold. But the US gold supply begins to shrink. In 1971, the gold standard ends.

Would you gamble with the gold standard?

The year is 1717. You are Sir Isaac Newton, famous scientist and warden of the Royal Mint. For centuries, Britain has been on a 'silver standard': its currency can be converted into silver at a fixed price. You alter the exchange rate between silver and gold coins, driving down the value of silver and putting Britain on a gold standard. Why did you do this? Some say you were influenced by your love of the yellow metal. After all, you are an alchemist: someone who aims to turn base metals into gold.

> It's not gold, but I can exchange it for gold.

> I can't exchange it for gold, but I can buy stuff with it.

REPRESENTATIVE MONEY is money that has value not because of what it's made of, but because it can be exchanged for something valuable, like gold.

FIAT MONEY. Today, we use fiat money. This has value not because it can be converted into gold or silver, but because governments *declare* that it has value.

Why do we love gold? Because it's rare, and also beautiful!

How it works

The 1848 Gold Rush increased the world gold supply, causing gold's value to drop. The world was on the gold standard, so this also caused a drop in the value of money.

What if your wealth becomes worthless?

You live in Germany in 1923. The country is in economic turmoil. There's a general strike and no goods are being made. When goods are scarce, sellers can charge higher prices, so money buys less – it loses its value. This is called inflation. Meanwhile, the government runs out of money, so it starts printing new notes. The flood of paper money turns inflation into 'hyperinflation'. By November, a single loaf of bread costs 200 billion marks. It is said that some people go shopping with a wheelbarrow piled high with money.

INFLATION. If money isn't linked to something finite like gold, there's nothing to stop governments from printing too much. Money's buying power falls and prices rise.

A HOUSE FOR A LOAF. During the German hyperinflation, one woman sold her house, planning to live on the money, but soon it wasn't enough to buy a loaf of bread.

Keep the money. I want the wheelbarrow.

Top tip

Suffering from hyperinflation? Try out these cures:
• Reduce the money supply.
• Stimulate economic growth.
• Peg the currency's value to other currencies, or gold.
• Abandon the currency, as Zimbabwe did.

At least it keeps me warm.

That will be a trillion dollars, please.

HUNGARY experienced the world's worst hyperinflation in 1945–1946. The government printed the largest-denomination banknote ever: 100 quintillion (that's 18 zeros) pengő.

ZIMBABWE suffered severe hyperinflation in 2007–2008, with prices doubling every 24 hours. Things got so bad, nurses and teachers couldn't even afford the bus fare to get to work.

23

Could you catch a counterfeiter?

It is 1925, and Alves dos Reis of Portugal has come up with a fiendish yet brilliant get-rich scheme. He has forged contracts from the governors of the Bank of Portugal authorising him to print banknotes for them. The printer, believing the contracts are genuine, has printed banknotes to the value of 290 million escudos, making Alves a very wealthy man. He goes on a massive spending spree. Then an investigator notices banknotes circulating with the same serial numbers. The game is up! The forger is arrested and sentenced to 20 years.

How did you get to be so rich, Alves?

I wanted to make mulberry jam.

I'll pay you to let me go.

Not with that money!

'Shover'
David Farnsworth in prison

FORGERY is as old as money itself. Early forgers would steal precious metal from coins to make new coins. Modern forgers have turned to copying banknotes.

CHINA. The first banknotes were made from mulberry wood. Guards were placed around mulberry forests to prevent forgers accessing the wood.

SHOVERS. During the American Revolutionary War, British forgers 'shoved' fake dollars into circulation to reduce the value of the US currency.

SUPERDOLLARS are very realistic fake US banknotes. Like official notes, they are printed on paper made from cotton and linen and contain a security thread and a watermark. Only experts can tell them apart.

Top tip

To foil the forgers, include the following on your banknotes:
• holograms
• embedded strips
• microprinting
• watermarks
• inks that change colour depending on the angle of the light.

Let's just say I made some money!

ALVES

25

Are you at ease with e-money?

You are a student living today. You carry cash to buy small items, like a cup of tea at the local café, but for everything else you use electronic money, or e-money. When you take the bus, you show an electronic travel card to a scanner, which deducts the fare from your account. You pay for groceries with a debit card, and buy books, games, clothes and other stuff online using a 'digital wallet'. Your rent gets paid automatically each month by direct debit. Money, for the most part, has become invisible.

I wish I could download some free money.

INTERNET BANKING. Today, all major banks offer an Internet service, so customers can manage their money and pay bills online.

ONLINE PAYMENTS.
The world's first secure online purchase was for a CD by the rock star Sting. It was carried out in the United States in August 1994.

I prefer the old sort of wallet.

DIGITAL WALLETS are electronic accounts used to make purchases online. They avoid the need to enter account details each time you buy, making transactions quicker and more secure.

CEASED TRADING DUE TO INTERNET

E-COMMERCE today accounts for 6 per cent of all retail sales. In some industries, like books, travel and music, the proportion is much higher, and is threatening brick-and-mortar shops.

Can you foretell the future of finance?

I t's twenty years in the future and you're shopping at your favourite store. You see a shirt you like and hold your smartphone near the label until you hear a beep. The shirt is now yours. There's no pay counter at the shop. The staff are there to help you find what you need, but payments are taken automatically. You paid with one of the new cryptocurrencies. As you head back into the mall you see a woman tossing something into a fountain. 'What was that?' you ask her. 'A coin,' she says. 'We used to use them for money. Now they're only good for making wishes.'

Happy birthday!

You're so romantic!

It's the house currency, Dad!

CONTACTLESS PAYMENT. People already use smartphones like credit cards, swiping barcodes to buy things. Soon we'll be able to send money to others by placing our phones close to each other.

CRYPTOCURRENCIES, such as Bitcoin, are backed by no government. Their value is based on their scarcity, as only a finite amount of the currency will ever be put into circulation.

LOCAL CURRENCIES such as London's Brixton Pound (available as paper notes and in electronic form) aim to stir economic activity in a particular town or area.

I didn't mean to buy this – my phone got too close.

Accidental contactless payments can happen, so:
• Keep your wallet at least 10 cm away from any card reader.
• Check your bank statements for unexpected payments.
• Consider buying a protective case for your cards.

Hello? Did someone order a tractor?

I just bought a virtual tractor!

VIRTUAL CURRENCIES are increasingly being used to buy things in games or apps. In the future, virtual currencies may start to become accepted in the real world.

COWRIES to cryptocurrencies. Money's come a long way since cowrie shells. But whatever form it takes, its function remains the same: it offers us a store of value and a medium of exchange.

29

Glossary

Bankrupt Judged by a court to be unable to pay one's debts.

Bill of exchange A document that binds one party to pay a fixed sum of money to another party at a predetermined future date.

Commodity money Money whose value comes from the commodity (raw material) of which it is made. A gold coin is an example of commodity money.

Counterfeit A fake – something made to imitate something valuable, such as a banknote, with the intention to deceive.

Credit The ability to obtain goods or services before payment, based on the trust that payment will be made in the future.

Credit card A small plastic card issued by a bank that allows the holder to buy goods or services on credit by electronic means.

Creditor A person or company to whom money is owed.

Currency A system of money in use in a particular country.

Debasement Reducing the value of something. With commodity money, coins can be debased by reducing the amount of precious metal they contain.

Debit card A card issued by a bank that allows the holder to transfer money electronically to another bank account when making a purchase.

Debt A sum of money that is owed.

Debtor A person or institution that owes a sum of money.

Denomination The face value of a banknote or coin.

E-commerce Buying and selling electronically on the Internet.

Exchange rate The value of one currency compared to another.

Fiat money Money which has value because the government says it has.

Forgery The copying of something valuable, such as a banknote, in order to deceive.

Gold standard A system by which the value of a currency is linked to the value of gold, and the currency can be exchanged for gold at a fixed rate.

Great Depression The economic slump that began in 1929 and continued for most of the 1930s. It was a time of low industrial productivity and trade, and high unemployment.

Indentured servant A debtor who agrees to work for his or her creditor until the debt is paid off.

Inflation A general increase in the prices of goods and services over a period of time.

Interest Money paid regularly by a borrower to a lender at a particular rate for the use of the money lent.

Mint To make coins by stamping metal; also, a place where coins are made.

Money supply The total amount of money in circulation in an economy.

Representative money Money whose value comes from being backed by a valuable commodity, such as gold. Countries that operate a gold standard use representative money.

Security (for a loan) Something valuable pledged or deposited as a guarantee that a loan will be repaid. If the borrower does not repay the loan, then the security is forfeited (it becomes the property of the lender).

Serial number A unique code number printed on a banknote or other object for identification purposes.

Tax Money that individuals and businesses are required to pay to the government to help it pay for things such as administration, security and public services.

Watermark A faint image made in some paper during manufacture, visible when held up to the light.

Index

Top ten richest people of all time

Here is a list of what is thought to be the richest human beings in history. Because they lived at different times and used different currencies, estimates of their wealth have been converted into present-day US dollars.

You may find other lists that disagree with this one, because there are different ways of calculating a person's wealth. For people who lived a long time ago, there is often no reliable information. That is why this list does not include fabulously wealthy ancient rulers such as Alexander the Great, Genghis Khan or King Solomon.

Name, occupation and dates	Approximate wealth ($)
1. Mansa Musa I, ruler of Mali Empire (c. 1280 – c. 1337)	400 billion
2. John D. Rockefeller, industrialist (1839–1937)	340 billion
3. Andrew Carnegie, steel tycoon (1835–1919)	310 billion
4. Tsar Nicholas II, ruler of Russia (1868–1918)	300 billion
5. Mir Osman Ali Khan, ruler of Hyderabad (1886–1967)	236 billion
6. William the Conqueror, king of England (c. 1028–1087)	230 billion
7. Jakob Fugger, banker (1459–1525)	221 billion
8. Muammar Gaddafi, ruler of Libya (1942–2011)	200 billion
9. Henry Ford, motor manufacturer (1863–1947)	199 billion
10. Cornelius Vanderbilt, transport magnate (1794–1877)	185 billion

The Rothschild banking dynasty

The Rothschilds may well be the richest family in human history, and they made their money through *money*, by investing, making loans and raising funds – banking, in other words. The founder of the dynasty was Mayer Amschel Rothschild, who set up a banking house in Frankfurt, Germany, in the 1760s. In the early 1800s, four of his sons left to establish banks in London, Vienna, Paris and Naples.

Global financiers

The Rothschild dynasty reached its height in the 19th century. By backing Britain in the Napoleonic Wars, the family helped bring down Napoleon. They went on to play a key role in the Industrial Revolution, funding the expansion of the railways and the building of the Suez Canal, as well as acquiring major interests in gold and diamond mines. In the 1820s, the Rothschilds helped create the country of Brazil by paying for its independence from Portugal. From 1852 they started making money in a literal sense: refining and casting coins for Britain's Royal Mint.

Setbacks and recovery

The Rothschilds suffered some big setbacks in the 20th century. In 1901 the Frankfurt bank was forced to close due to the lack of a male heir. The stock market crash of 1929 was another serious blow. Then, in 1938, the Austrian Rothschilds' interests were seized by the Nazis. But the firm recovered and is still a powerful international bank today. It now operates as a single organisation with about 2,800 employees in 40 countries around the world. Its assets are worth an estimated $350 billion.

Did you know?

- The word *money* comes from the Roman goddess Juno Moneta, protector of funds. In ancient Rome, money was minted near her temple.

- The tally stick system, set up by King Henry I of England in about 1110, lasted until 1826. In 1834, the tallies, stored in the Palace of Westminster, were ordered to be burned. Unfortunately, the fire got out of control and most of the palace buildings burned down.

- The world's first overdraft was offered to William Hog, a merchant, in 1728. The Royal Bank of Scotland allowed him to take £1,000 more out of his account than he had in it.

- The world's first cashpoint machine (ATM) was opened in Enfield, North London, in 1967. The first person to use it was the English comedy actor Reg Varney.

- During the American Civil War, counterfeit currency became a major problem: more than a third of all bills in circulation were believed to be fakes.

- Queen Elizabeth II's portrait appears on the currencies of 33 different countries – more than any other individual. Her image first appeared in 1935, when Canada included the 9-year-old princess on its $20 notes.

- Paper money can carry more germs than a household toilet. Most viruses and bacteria can survive on banknotes for about 48 hours, but paper money can transmit a live flu virus for up to 17 days.